LE CORDON BLEU

HOME COLLECTION

TARTS & PASTRIES

PERIPLUS
EDITIONS

contents

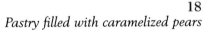

recipe ratings ✿ *easy* ✿✿ *a little more care needed* ✿✿✿ *more care needed*

Pecan tart

This French version of the classic Southern pecan pie uses a rich, sweet pastry baked in the distinctive tart pan. The filling, however, remains the same—simply superb—especially when served with whipped cream.

Preparation time **20 minutes + 30 minutes resting**
Total cooking time **50 minutes**
Serves 6–8

3/4 quantity sweet pastry
  (see page 59)

FILLING
2 eggs
pinch of salt
2 tablespoons unsalted butter, melted
2/3 cup light corn syrup
2/3 cup lightly packed dark brown sugar
I teaspoon vanilla extract
I cup pecans, coarsely chopped

1 Preheat the oven to 325°F. Roll the dough out to 1/8-inch thick and line a 1-inch deep, 9-inch fluted tart pan with removable bottom (see Chef's techniques, page 63).

2 To make the filling, beat the eggs in a bowl. Add the salt, butter, corn syrup, brown sugar and vanilla and mix until well combined.

3 Sprinkle the pecans over the base of the pastry shell, then pour in the filling. Bake for 45–50 minutes, or until the filling has just set. If the filling puffs up too much, reduce the oven temperature to 300°F.

4 Leave in the pan for 5 minutes, or until cool enough to handle. Remove to a wire rack and cool completely.

Chef's tip The pecans can be left whole or use almost any nut, such as walnuts, hazelnuts or macadamias.

Millefeuille

Millefeuille, meaning "a thousand leaves," refers to the layers of puff pastry used in this recipe. Filled with a delicious vanilla cream, a millefeuille may be served as one large pastry or cut into individual portions.

Preparation time 1 hour + 15 minutes resting
Total cooking time 40 minutes
Serves 6

1 quantity puff pastry (see pages 60–61)
strawberries, to garnish
confectioners' sugar, to dust

PASTRY CREAM
3 cups milk
1 vanilla bean, split lengthwise
9 egg yolks
3/4 cup sugar
2/3 cup all-purpose flour
1/3 cup cornstarch

1 Preheat the oven to 425°F. Divide the dough in half and roll each piece into a square, 1/8-inch thick. Place one square on a buttered baking sheet lined with wax paper, and pierce all over with a fork to stop the dough from rising too much. Let the pastry rest in the refrigerator for 15 minutes. Before baking, cover the pastry with a second sheet of wax paper and another baking sheet. Bake for 10–15 minutes. Flip the pastry over and bake for 10 minutes more, or until light golden all over. Remove the top baking sheet and paper and let cool on a wire rack. Repeat with the other square.

2 To make the pastry cream, place the milk and vanilla bean in a saucepan and bring to a boil. In a bowl, whisk the egg yolks with the sugar until light in color. Sift in the flour and cornstarch and whisk until blended. Remove and discard the vanilla bean. Pour half the boiling milk into the yolk mixture, whisk well, then return the mixture to the saucepan of milk. Bring to a boil, stirring constantly, and boil for 1 minute to completely cook the flour. Remove from the heat and spread the pastry cream on a tray to cool quickly. Cover the surface with wax paper to prevent a skin forming.

3 Trim the edges of the cooked pastry with a serrated knife and reserve the trimmings, then cut each square in half. Save the neatest piece for the top. Whisk the cooled pastry cream until smooth. Pipe or spoon a third of the cream onto a piece of puff pastry, cover with a second piece of pastry and pipe the second third of the cream on top. Repeat with the third piece of pastry and remaining cream. Place the last piece of pastry on top and press lightly. Smooth any cream that comes out of the sides with a flexible metal spatula, and fill any holes. Crush the pastry trimmings and press onto the sides. Decorate with the strawberries and dust with sifted confectioners' sugar.

Individual Paris Brest

These wheel-shaped cream-puff pastry cakes were made in honor of a bicycle race that took place between Paris and Brest, a town on the Brittany coast.

*Preparation time **45 minutes***
*Total cooking time **45 minutes***
Makes 4

I quantity cream-puff pastry
  (see page 62)
I egg, beaten, to glaze
1/2 cup sliced or chopped almonds

PRALINE PASTRY CREAM
I cup milk
I teaspoon vanilla extract
2 egg yolks
1/4 cup sugar
2 tablespoons all-purpose flour
2 tablespoons cornstarch
I 1/4 oz. praline paste or chocolate hazelnut spread
1/3 cup unsalted butter, at room temperature

1 Preheat the oven to 350°F. Butter a baking sheet and chill until the butter sets. Dip a 4-inch round cutter in flour and mark four circles on the baking sheet. Leave a 2 inch gap between each circle.

2 Spoon the cream-puff pastry into a pastry bag fitted with a 1/2-inch round or star nozzle. Using the floured marks as a guide, pipe the mixture into perfect rings. Lightly brush with a little beaten egg, being careful not to let it drip down the sides as this may prevent the dough from rising evenly. Use the brush, if necessary, to seal the seam of the ring and smooth out the edges. Sprinkle with the almonds and bake for 35 minutes, or until crisp and golden. Remove from the baking sheet while still hot and cool on a wire rack.

3 To make the praline pastry cream, place the milk and vanilla in a saucepan and bring slowly to a boil. In a bowl, whisk the egg yolks with the sugar until light in color. Sift in the flour and cornstarch and whisk until blended. Pour half the boiling milk into the yolk mixture, whisk well, then return the mixture to the saucepan of milk. Bring to a boil, stirring constantly, and boil for 1 minute to completely cook the flour. Remove from the heat and spread the pastry cream on a tray to cool quickly. Cover the surface with waxed paper to prevent a skin forming. Once cooled, beat in the praline paste, then whisk in the butter. Continue to whisk until the cream has lightened in color and appears fluffy. Set the cream aside.

4 Split each ring of cream-puff pastry in half horizontally. Spoon the praline pastry cream into a pastry bag and pipe it onto the bottom halves. Replace the tops on the rings and serve.

Exotic fruit tartlets

Individual fruit tartlets filled with fresh pastry cream and soft fruit are a feature at every French bakery. These tartlets are made with delicious tropical fruit, however any seasonal fruit could be used.

Preparation time 40 minutes + 20 minutes refrigeration
Total cooking time 25 minutes
Makes 6

I quantity sweet pastry
   (see page 59)
I pineapple, peeled and cut into chunks
2 kiwi fruit, peeled and cut into chunks
I papaya, peeled and cut into chunks
I mango, peeled and cut into chunks
4 Cape gooseberries (physalis), husks removed and cut
   in half (optional)
pulp of 2 passion fruit
5 lychees (litchi), peeled and seeded
I carambola (star fruit), cut into slices and seeded

PASTRY CREAM
1 1/2 cups milk
I vanilla bean, split lengthwise
4 egg yolks
1/3 cup sugar
2 1/2 tablespoons all-purpose flour
2 1/2 tablespoons cornstarch

1 Brush six individual fluted tart pans, about 3 inches across the bottom, with melted butter.
2 Roll out the pastry on a floured surface about 1/8-inch thick. Cut out six 4-inch rounds and line the pans (see Chef's techniques, page 63). Refrigerate for 20 minutes. Preheat the oven to 350°F.
3 Bake blind for 10 minutes until firm. Remove the weights and paper and return the pastry shells to the oven for a further 10 minutes, or until the center of the pastry begins to color (see Chef's techniques, page 63). Let cool for 2 minutes, then remove the shells from the pans and place on a wire rack to cool completely.
4 To make the pastry cream, place the milk and vanilla in a saucepan and bring slowly to a boil. In a bowl, whisk the egg yolks with the sugar until light in color. Sift in the flour and cornstarch and whisk until blended. Remove and discard the vanilla bean. Pour half the boiling milk into the yolk mixture, whisk well, then return the mixture to the saucepan of milk. Bring to a boil, stirring constantly, and boil for 1 minute to completely cook the flour. Remove from the heat and spread the pastry cream on a tray to cool quickly. Cover the surface with waxed paper to prevent a skin forming. Set aside to cool. Whisk until smooth before using.
5 Mix the prepared fruit in a bowl and set aside. Fill each tart three-quarters full with the pastry cream, level the surface, then pile the fruit on top. Each tart should look luxuriantly full of fruit.

Chef's tip If preferred, this could be made as one large tart using an 8-inch fluted tart pan with removable bottom. Chill the tart for 1 hour before serving, to settle the fruit and make it easier to cut.

Lemon tart

This lemon tart is the perfect end to any meal, with just the right balance of tangy lemon and sweetness. Try substituting other citrus fruits such as orange or lime, or a combination of two fruits.

Preparation time **30 minutes + refrigeration**
Total cooking time **50 minutes**
Serves 8

I quantity sweet pastry (see page 59)
confectioners' sugar, to dust

FILLING
2/3 cup heavy cream
4 eggs
2/3 cup sugar
juice of 4 lemons, about 3/4 cup
finely grated rind of I lemon

1 Brush a 1 1/2-inch deep, 8-inch fluted tart pan with removable bottom, with melted butter.
2 On a floured surface, roll out the pastry into a circle about 1/4-inch thick, and line the tart pan (see Chef's techniques, page 63). Chill for 30 minutes. Preheat the oven to 375°F. Bake blind for 10 minutes until the pastry is firm. Remove the weights and paper and if the bottom of the pastry looks wet, continue baking for 3–4 minutes (see Chef's techniques, page 63). Reduce the heat to 275°F.
3 To make the filling, warm the cream in a small saucepan over low heat. In a large bowl, whisk together the eggs, sugar and lemon juice. Stir in the warmed cream. Pass the mixture through a fine sieve, then stir in the grated lemon rind and pour into the pastry shell. Bake for 35 minutes, or until the filling is just firm to the touch. When the tart comes out of the oven it will appear quite soft in the middle. Let cool completely, then remove from the pan and chill for several hours or overnight, until the filling is firm enough to cut. Dust with sifted confectioners' sugar just before serving.

Chef's tip Keep refrigerated and use within 3 days.

Chocolate éclairs

In French, éclair *means literally "lightning." The name of these filled cream-puff pastry buns is probably due to the fact that they rarely last long!*

*Preparation time **1 hour***
*Total cooking time **1 hour 15 minutes***
*Makes **12***

1 quantity cream-puff pastry (see page 62)
1 beaten egg, to glaze

PASTRY CREAM
1 cup milk
1 teaspoon vanilla extract
2 egg yolks
1/4 cup sugar
2 tablespoons all-purpose flour
2 tablespoons cornstarch

CHOCOLATE GANACHE
3 oz. semisweet chocolate, chopped into small pieces
1/3 cup whipping cream

1 Preheat the oven to 350°F. Grease a baking sheet with softened butter and chill until set.
2 Fill a pastry bag fitted with a medium plain nozzle with the cream-puff pastry. Pipe the mixture to form 3–4 inch logs on the baking sheet. Lightly brush with the beaten egg. Take care not to let any of the egg drip down the sides as this may prevent the dough from rising evenly. Press gently with a fork. Bake for 30–35 minutes, or until crisp and golden. Immediately remove from the baking sheet and cool on a wire rack.

3 To make the pastry cream, place the milk and vanilla in a saucepan and bring slowly to a boil. In a bowl, whisk the egg yolks with the sugar until light in color. Sift in the flour and cornstarch and whisk until blended. Pour half the boiling milk into the yolk mixture, whisk well, then return the mixture to the saucepan of milk. Bring to a boil, stirring constantly, then boil for 1 minute to completely cook the flour. Remove from the heat and spread the pastry cream on a tray to cool quickly. Cover the surface with waxed paper to prevent a skin forming. Let cool completely.
4 To make the chocolate ganache, place the chocolate in a small bowl. Bring the cream to a boil in a small saucepan and pour it over the chocolate. Wait a few seconds, then gently stir until the chocolate is completely melted and smooth.
5 Using the tip of a small sharp knife, make a small hole at one end on the underside of each éclair. Place the cooled pastry cream in a bowl and whisk until smooth, then spoon the cream into a pastry bag fitted with a small nozzle. Push the tip into one of the holes and fill the entire cavity with the pastry cream. Hold the éclair in the palm of your hand and stop adding the filling just at the moment you can feel it expanding. A little of the cream will ooze out once the nozzle is removed; wipe this off.
6 Using a small knife or metal spatula, carefully spread the chocolate ganache over the tops of the éclairs. Allow the éclairs to stand in a cool place until the ganache has set.

Brioche plum tart

This delicious tart is made from a soft brioche dough and filled with a vanilla cream and fresh ripe plums.
Perfect for brunch or served at the end of a summer party.

Preparation time 45 minutes + overnight refrigeration
Total cooking time 45 minutes
Serves 6

BRIOCHE DOUGH
1 1/4 cups bread or all-purpose flour
1/2 teaspoon salt
1 tablespoon sugar
2 teaspoons milk
1 1/2 teaspoons fresh yeast
  or 1 teaspoon dry yeast
2 eggs, lightly beaten
1/4 cup unsalted butter, at room temperature

PASTRY CREAM
2 cups milk
1/2 vanilla bean, split lengthwise
5 egg yolks
1/2 cup sugar
2 1/2 tablespoons all-purpose flour
2 1/2 tablespoons cornstarch

3–5 plums, about 8 oz., halved and pitted
1/4 cup apricot jam

1 To make the brioche dough, sift the flour and salt into a large bowl, stir in the sugar and make a well in the center. Heat the milk in a saucepan until lukewarm; remove from the heat. Add the yeast, stir until dissolved and pour into the dry ingredients. Add the eggs and beat to make an elastic dough (do this using your hand, with fingers slightly apart and a slapping motion from the wrist, or, with the dough hook attachment on an electric mixer). Place the butter in a bowl, soften it with a wooden spoon and add to the dough in three or four batches. Continue to beat until the dough is smooth and has a silky shine. Place the dough in a large bowl that has been sprinkled with flour to prevent sticking. Cover loosely with oiled plastic wrap and refrigerate for at least 8 hours or overnight. Grease a 1-inch deep, 8-inch fluted tart pan with removable bottom, with softened butter and set aside.

2 Punch the dough down, folding the sides toward the center. Remove from the bowl and knead for 1 minute on a lightly floured surface. Roll out into a 1/8–1/4-inch thick circle. Line the tart pan with the dough (see Chef's techniques, page 63). Chill for 20 minutes. Preheat the oven to 325°F.

3 To make the pastry cream, place the milk and vanilla bean in a saucepan and bring slowly to a boil. In a bowl, whisk the egg yolks with the sugar until light in color. Sift in the flour and cornstarch and whisk until blended. Remove and discard the vanilla bean. Pour half the boiling milk into the yolk mixture, whisk well, then return the mixture to the saucepan of milk. Bring to a boil, stirring constantly, and boil for 1 minute to completely cook the flour. Remove from the heat and spread the pastry cream on a tray to cool quickly. Cover the surface with waxed paper to prevent a skin forming and leave to cool. Whisk the pastry cream until smooth before using.

4 Spread the pastry cream over the brioche and arrange the plums, cut-side-down, on top. Bake for 40 minutes, or until the brioche is crisp and golden. Cool on a wire rack before removing from the pan. Heat the apricot jam with 1 tablespoon water until melted. Bring to a boil, then strain and brush over the plums to glaze.

Pastry filled with caramelized pears

A hot pastry made from two strips of puff pastry enclosing a filling is known in France as a dartois *and is said to have been named after a famous vaudeville artist of the nineteenth century, François-Victor Dartois.*

*Preparation time **30 minutes + 30 minutes chilling***
*Total cooking time **50 minutes***
Serves 4

I quantity puff pastry (see pages 60–61)
I egg, beaten, to glaze
1/3 cup apricot jam

FILLING
7 small pears, about I 1/4 lb.
2 tablespoons unsalted butter
1/4 cup sugar
pinch of ground cinnamon

1 Divide the puff pastry in half. Roll out one half and trim into a rectangle 4 inches wide, 12 inches long, and 1/8-inch thick. Roll out the other half of dough to a rectangle 5 inches wide and 13 inches long. Place on two baking sheets lined with waxed paper and refrigerate.
2 Peel, core and cut the pears into 1/2-inch cubes. Melt the butter in a nonstick skillet. Add the pears and toss until coated with butter. Sprinkle with sugar, mix well and cook until caramelized and tender. Remove from the heat. Stir in the cinnamon. Pour the mixture into a colander or strainer placed over a bowl and set aside to drain and cool. Preheat the oven to 350°F.
3 Brush the top of the smaller piece of pastry with some of the egg. Do not allow the egg to drip down the edges. Arrange the pears down the center of the pastry, being careful not to get any too near the edges. Place the other larger piece of pastry on top and press the edges with your fingertips, or a knife, to seal. Brush the top with egg and chill for 30 minutes.
4 Brush the pastry a second time with the beaten egg, then using the back of a sharp pointed knife, lightly draw a crisscross design on the top. Bake for 40 minutes, or until the bottom is light golden and uniform in color (check this by gently lifting up the side of the pastry with a wide metal spatula). Cool on a wire rack.
5 Heat the apricot jam with a tablespoon of water. When the jam has melted, strain the glaze and lightly brush the top of the pastry. Serve whole or cut into individual portions.

Bitter chocolate tart

A deliciously rich tart ideally complemented by some whipped cream and a handful of fresh berries.

Preparation time **40–45 minutes + cooling**
Total cooking time **50 minutes**
Serves 6–8

1 quantity sweet pastry (see page 59)
5 oz. bittersweet or semisweet chocolate, chopped
2/3 cup unsalted butter, chopped
4 eggs
3/4 cup sugar
2/3 cup all-purpose flour
unsweetened cocoa, to dust

1 Preheat the oven to 400°F. Roll out the pastry 1/8-inch thick and line a greased shallow 10-inch fluted tart pan with removable bottom (see Chef's techniques, page 63).

2 Bake blind for 10 minutes until firm. Remove the weights and paper and return to the oven for a further 5 minutes (see Chef's techniques, page 63).

3 Heat the chocolate and butter in the top of a double boiler over steaming water, making sure that the base of the insert does not touch the water. Stir until melted and smooth, then remove from the heat. Beat the eggs, sugar and flour together, then stir the mixture into the melted chocolate and butter. Pour this mixture into the pastry shell and bake for 20–25 minutes, or until the filling is just set.

4 Remove the tart from the pan and let cool completely before dusting with sifted cocoa.

Band of fruits

This is a very simple dessert to prepare yet it looks impressive and has a wonderfully fresh flavor.
Experiment with a variety of soft fruits to suit your taste and the seasons.

*Preparation time **1 hour + refrigeration***
*Total cooking time **25 minutes***
Serves 6–8

🌼

1 quantity puff pastry (see pages 60–61)
1 egg, lightly beaten, to glaze
1 lb. strawberries, hulled and sliced
2 kiwi fruits, peeled and sliced
1/4 cup apricot jam

PASTRY CREAM
2 cups milk
1/2 vanilla bean, split lengthwise
5 egg yolks
1/2 cup sugar
2 1/2 tablespoons all-purpose flour
2 1/2 tablespoons cornstarch
1 tablespoon Grand Marnier

1 Preheat the oven to 400°F. Roll out the pastry on a lightly floured surface to a 13 1/2 x 9-inch rectangle and place on a greased baking sheet. Trim the edges with a sharp knife, then cut two 1 1/4-inch wide strips from the long side of the rectangle and set aside, taking care not to stretch the pastry. Brush the long sides of the rectangle with the beaten egg in a 1 1/4-inch wide strip, then lay the cut strips on top. Using the back of a knife, make crosshatch score marks on these outer strips, then brush lightly with the beaten egg. Pierce the base of the pastry with a fork and chill for 20 minutes. Bake for 15–20 minutes, or until the pastry has risen and is golden brown. Cool on a wire rack.

2 To make the pastry cream, place the milk and vanilla bean in a saucepan and bring slowly to a boil. In a bowl, whisk the egg yolks with the sugar until light in color. Sift in the flour and cornstarch and whisk until blended. Remove and discard the vanilla bean. Pour half the boiling milk into the yolk mixture, whisk well, then return the mixture to the saucepan of milk. Bring to a boil, stirring constantly, and boil for 1 minute to completely cook the flour. Remove from the heat and pour into a bowl, stir in the Grand Marnier and cover the surface with waxed paper to prevent a skin forming. Refrigerate until cold.

3 To assemble the dessert, stir the chilled pastry cream briefly to loosen it, then pipe or spoon the cream onto the pastry base to fill the space between the two pastry strips. Smooth the surface of the cream with the back of a spoon and arrange the strawberry slices on top, alternating with the kiwi fruit. Make sure that the cream does not show through. In a small saucepan, melt the apricot jam with 1 tablespoon water to make a smooth liquid. Strain the glaze and dab it lightly over the fruit, without covering the same area twice. This will create a glossy shine. To serve, cut the pastry crosswise into slices.

Chef's tips Piping the pastry cream is quicker than spooning, it also gives a more even distribution.

Fill the brush well when using the apricot glaze so that the glaze falls into place easily without leaving any streaky brush marks.

Pumpkin tart

While pumpkin pie is the traditional favorite served with Thanksgiving dinner, this version is also a treat after any cold weather meal. It has a warm, spicy aroma and is delicious served with sweetened whipped cream.

*Preparation time **20 minutes + refrigeration***
*Total cooking time **45 minutes***
Serves 6–8

1/2 quantity sweet pastry (see page 59)

FILLING
3/4 cup pumpkin purée (see Chef's tips)
2 eggs
3 tablespoons sugar
large pinch salt
small pinch of ground cloves
small pinch of ground cinnamon
small pinch of ground nutmeg
small pinch of ground ginger
2 tablespoons heavy cream

1 Brush a shallow, 8-inch fluted tart pan with removable bottom, with melted butter.
2 Roll out the pastry on a floured surface to a circle about 1/8-inch thick and line the tart pan (see Chef's techniques, page 63). Refrigerate for 30 minutes.
3 Preheat the oven to 375°F. Bake blind for 10 minutes until the pastry is firm. Remove the weights and paper and bake for 5–10 minutes more, or until the center begins to color (see Chef's techniques, page 63). Allow to cool. Reduce the oven temperature to 325°F.
4 To make the filling, place the pumpkin purée, eggs, sugar, salt, spices and cream in a bowl and whisk until smooth and blended. Pour into the pastry shell. Bake for 25–30 minutes, or until the filling is firm to the touch. Allow to cool slightly, then remove from the pan and transfer to a serving plate. Serve the tart warm, cut into wedges, or if you prefer to serve it cold, allow the tart to cool, then chill for at least 30 minutes.

Chef's tips Pumpkin purée is available canned, but to prepare a delicious alternative, take 10 oz. butternut or hubbard squash, peel and cut it into pieces, remove the seeds, and place in a saucepan. Barely cover with cold water and add 1/4 cup sugar. Bring to a simmer, cover and simmer until the squash is tender. Drain well and purée the squash in a blender, food processor or by pressing it through a strainer.

If serving the tart cold, add shine to the surface with an apricot glaze: Melt 1/4 cup apricot jam with 1 tablespoon water until liquid. Strain, then brush the glaze across the surface, avoiding going over the same area twice to prevent streaks.

To give the pastry added crunch, try stirring 1/4 cup chopped walnuts into the dry ingredients before mixing.

Cream-puff pastry swans

These elegant cream-puff pastry swans make a light and very impressive dessert. Any fruit may be substituted for the red berries when they are out of season.

*Preparation time **1 hour***
*Total cooking time **50 minutes***
Makes 4

❋ ❋

1 quantity cream-puff pastry (see page 62)
1 beaten egg, to glaze
fresh red berries, to garnish
confectioners' sugar, to dust

CHANTILLY CREAM
1 1/2 cups whipping cream, chilled
3/4 cup confectioners' sugar
1 teaspoon vanilla extract

1 Preheat the oven to 350°F. Spoon the cream-puff pastry into a pastry bag fitted with a large plain nozzle. Pipe thick oval balls, about the size of an egg, onto a buttered baking sheet (these will be the bodies of the swans). Brush very lightly with the beaten egg. Bake for 35–40 minutes, or until the pastry is well colored. Remove from the baking sheet and cool on a wire rack.

2 Using a pastry bag fitted with a 1/4-inch round plain nozzle, pipe large question marks (minus the dots) onto a baking sheet lined with wax paper (these will be the necks of the swans). Weigh down the corners of the paper or stick them down with a little of the dough. Bake for 10–15 minutes, or until the pastry is well colored. Make sure that they are dry or they will not hold up when assembled. Transfer to a wire rack to allow to cool.

3 To make the Chantilly cream, pour the cream into a bowl and add the confectioners' sugar and vanilla. Using a whisk or electric mixer, beat the cream until it just forms soft peaks.

4 Cut the top third off the tops of the bodies and scrape out any uncooked pastry from inside. Then cut the tops diagonally to shape two triangles. Spoon the Chantilly cream into a pastry bag with a medium star nozzle and fill the bodies. Carefully place a triangle of pastry on each side to make the wings of the swans and gently push the necks into one end of the bodies. Finally, fill with the red berries and dust with sifted confectioners' sugar to serve.

Crème brûlée tart

A delicious variation on the all-time favorite, crème brûlée. Gently pierce the firm caramelized top to discover the soft creamy interior.

Preparation time 20 minutes + refrigeration
Total cooking time 1 hour 10 minutes
Serves 6

1/2 **quantity sweet pastry (see page 59)**
3/4 **cup heavy cream**
1/4 **cup milk**
4 **egg yolks**
2 **tablespoons sugar**
I **teaspoon vanilla extract**
2 1/2 **tablespoons sugar, extra, to glaze**

1 Brush a shallow, 8-inch fluted tart pan with removable bottom, with melted butter. Roll out the pastry on a floured surface to a circle about 1/8-inch thick. Line the tart pan (see Chef's techniques, page 63), then chill for 30 minutes. Preheat the oven to 375°F.

2 Bake blind for 10 minutes until the pastry is firm. Remove the weights and paper and bake for a further 5–10 minutes, or until the center begins to color (see Chef's techniques, page 63). Cool on a wire rack. Reduce the oven temperature to 250°F.

3 Pour the cream and milk into a small saucepan and bring to a boil. In a bowl, whisk together the egg yolks and sugar. While whisking, slowly add the boiling liquid, then the vanilla. Strain the mixture into the pastry shell. Bake for 45 minutes, or until the filling is set and firm to the light touch of a finger. Cool the tart completely.

4 Preheat the broiler to medium and sprinkle the top of the tart filling evenly with the extra sugar. Cover the edge of the pastry with a strip of foil and place under the broiler to caramelize. If any areas are browning too quickly, cover loosely with foil. Carefully remove the tart from its pan, being careful not to touch the hot sugar, and let cool.

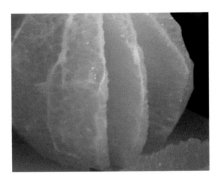

Orange tart

This caramelized orange tart with its creamy filling is quick to make and always popular served either plain or with a little whipped cream.

Preparation time 20 minutes + refrigeration
Total cooking time 30 minutes
Serves 6–8

❉ ❉

I quantity sweet pastry (see page 59)
I tablespoon sugar
2 oranges

ORANGE FILLING
3/4 cup unsalted butter
finely grated rind of 1/2 orange
I 1/4 cups sugar
4 eggs
6 egg yolks
1/4 cup cornstarch
1/2 cup orange juice

1 Preheat the oven to 350°F. Grease a shallow, 9-inch fluted tart pan with removable bottom, with melted butter. Roll out the pastry 1/8 inch thick and line the tart pan (see Chef's techniques, page 63).

2 Bake blind for 10 minutes until firm. Remove the weights and paper and bake for 15 minutes more, or until the pastry is lightly colored (see Chef's techniques, page 63). Transfer to a wire rack and let cool.

3 To make the orange filling, melt the butter in a saucepan, add the orange rind and gently heat through. Remove from the heat and set aside. In a bowl, whisk the sugar, eggs and egg yolks together until pale in color. Sift in the cornstarch and mix well, then add the orange juice. Add the egg mixture to the butter and orange rind and place the pan over medium-high heat. Stirring constantly, bring to a boil. Remove from the heat and pour into a shallow dish. Cover the surface with waxed paper and refrigerate until cold.

4 Preheat the broiler to moderate, beat the orange filling until smooth, spread into the pastry shell and smooth the top. Sprinkle with the sugar, cover the edge of the pastry with a strip of foil and place the tart under the broiler to caramelize. Allow to cool, then chill the tart.

5 Cut the top and bottom off one orange. Place one cut end on the cutting board and cut from top to bottom with a sharp knife, following the contour of the orange and cutting off just enough peel and pith to expose the flesh. Slice off any pith remaining and, holding the orange in one hand, carefully cut between the membrane and flesh to remove the segments. Repeat with the second orange. Place two orange segments on each slice just before serving. You can serve some whipped cream alongside topped with orange peel.

Apple turnovers

Served hot or cold, these turnovers are good to eat at any time of the day. In France, apple is the traditional filling, however they could be made with any fruit compote or pie filling.

Preparation time **40 minutes**
Total cooking time **35 minutes**
Makes 8–10

❂ ❂

I quantity puff pastry (see pages 60–61)
I egg, beaten, to glaze
1/4 cup sugar

APPLE COMPOTE
2 tablespoons unsalted butter
2 tablespoons sugar
2 apples, peeled and cored, cut into 1/4-inch cubes
juice of 1/4 lemon
pinch of vanilla sugar (see Chef's tip)
pinch of ground cinnamon

1 Roll out the puff pastry about 1/4-inch thick. Cut out 8–10 circles using a 5-inch fluted cutter. Roll each circle into an oval 5 inches wide and 8 inches long. Place on a baking sheet lined with waxed paper and chill.

2 To make the apple compote, melt the butter and sugar in a heavy-bottomed skillet over medium heat and cook until lightly colored. Add the apple and sauté for 2 minutes. Add the lemon juice, vanilla sugar, cinnamon and 3 tablespoons water. Bring to a boil and simmer for 5 minutes, stirring occasionally, until the water evaporates. Spread the mixture on a plate to cool.

3 Preheat the oven to 400°F. Place the ovals of pastry on a floured surface. Brush the edges with the egg. Divide the apple compote between the ovals. Fold each piece of pastry in half over the filling to make a semicircular turnover and press the edges lightly to seal. Place the turnovers on a baking sheet, brush the tops with the egg and lightly score the tops using the back of a small knife.

4 Make a syrup by mixing the sugar and 1/4 cup water in a small saucepan. Stir over medium heat until the sugar dissolves, bring to a boil, then remove from the heat and cool.

5 Bake the turnovers for 5 minutes, then reduce the temperature to 350°F and bake for 15–20 minutes more. Brush with the syrup and allow to cool on a wire rack. Serve warm or cold.

Chef's tip It is easy to make your own vanilla sugar. Just place a fresh vanilla bean inside a jar of sugar. Seal well and use whenever required.

Butter streusel tart

Streusel, the German word for "sprinkle," *refers to a crumb topping that has become a favorite in many countries. In this recipe, the crumbly texture provides a good contrast to the creamy filling.*

Preparation time **1 hour + 30 minutes refrigeration**
Total cooking time **35 minutes**
Serves 6–8

DOUGH
2/3 cup milk
1/2 oz. fresh yeast or 1/4 oz. dry yeast
2 1/4 cups all-purpose flour
1/2 teaspoon salt
2 tablespoons sugar
finely grated rind of 1/2 lemon
I egg, lightly beaten
3 tablespoons unsalted butter, melted

FILLING
1/2 cup milk
I vanilla bean, split lengthwise
2 1/2 tablespoons cornstarch
1/4 cup sugar
3 oz. cream cheese
finely grated rind of 1/2 lemon
I tablespoon rum

STREUSEL TOPPING
1/2 cup all-purpose flour
2 tablespoons chilled unsalted butter, cut up
2 tablespoons sugar

1 Grease a shallow, 8-inch fluted tart pan with removable bottom, with butter and refrigerate.
2 To make the dough, heat the milk until lukewarm, remove from the heat, add the yeast and stir until dissolved. Sift the flour and salt into a bowl, add the sugar and lemon rind and make a well in the center.

Pour in the egg, melted butter and milk mixture. Bring the ingredients together with your hands, then knead for 10–15 minutes to make a soft dough, adding more flour if it starts to feel sticky. Cover with plastic wrap and chill for 30 minutes.

3 On a floured surface, using a floured rolling pin, roll the dough out to a circle 1/4-inch thick. Line the tart pan (see Chef's techniques, page 63). Refrigerate while preparing the filling. Preheat the oven to 400°F.

4 To make the filling, place the milk in a saucepan and add the vanilla bean. Bring slowly to a boil, then remove from the heat. Sift the cornstarch into a small bowl, then mix to a paste with a little cold water. Strain the milk into the cornstarch, discarding the vanilla bean, and stir until smooth. Return the mixture to the saucepan and bring to a boil, stirring constantly. Cook for 30 seconds, or until the mixture boils and thickens. Remove from the heat and cool. Cream together the sugar, cream cheese, lemon rind and rum in a bowl. Add the cooled thickened milk to the cheese mixture, beat well until blended and set aside to cool. Spoon the filling into the pastry shell and smooth the surface with a flexible metal spatula.

5 To make the streusel topping, place the flour and butter in a bowl and rub the mixture together until it resembles fine bread crumbs, then stir in the sugar. Sprinkle this mixture over the top of the filling and bake for 25–30 minutes, or until golden brown.

6 Cool the tart slightly in the pan, then gently lift out and cool on a wire rack. Decorate with thin shreds of lemon or orange rind if desired.

Chef's tip For a variation, place chopped fruit on top of the filling before sprinkling with the topping. Plums, cherries and pears work well.

Praline tart

The almonds used in this tart were originally a speciality of Montargis in France. Today, however, they have become traditional in French fairgrounds, where they are cooked in the open air in copper pans.

*Preparation time **45 minutes + 15 minutes refrigeration***
*Total cooking time **45 minutes***
Serves 6–8

🌼 🌼 🌼

1 quantity sweet pastry (see page 59)
1 egg, beaten with a few drops of water
1¼ cups heavy cream
12 oz. candied almonds, finely chopped
confectioners' sugar, to dust

1 Preheat the oven to 350°F. Grease a shallow, 9-inch fluted tart pan with removable bottom, with butter and refrigerate. Roll the dough into a large circle, ⅛-inch thick. Line the tart pan (see Chef's techniques, page 63), then refrigerate for about 15 minutes.
2 Bake blind for 10 minutes until firm. Remove the weights and paper, brush the inside of the pastry shell with the beaten egg, allow to dry and then brush with a second coat. Bake for 10 minutes more, or until the pastry is evenly browned (see Chef's techniques, page 63).
3 Fill a shallow pan with cold water and place it next to the stove. In a heavy-bottomed saucepan, mix the cream and chopped pralines or almonds. Cook over medium-high heat, stirring occasionally to prevent burning. Using a sugar thermometer, heat the mixture to 242°F–248°F, the firm ball stage, then immediately place the saucepan into the pan of cold water. To test the temperature without a thermometer: As the mixture begins to thicken, dip in the tip of a small knife then dip the knife into a bowl of water. If it is ready, the mixture can be shaped to a malleable ball when pulled off the knife. If it dissolves or does not hold its shape, it needs to continue cooking. Do not overcook or it will set too hard.
4 Let the mixture stand for 1 minute to let the air bubbles come to the surface. Pour into the cooked pastry shell and cool to room temperature. Dust with sifted confectioners' sugar before serving.

Chef's tip If you are not using a sugar thermometer you must be very careful once the mixture starts to thicken and darken in color—it will heat quickly and is very easily overcooked. Prepare the cold water before starting to cook and be very careful when handling sugar, do not dip your fingers into it or allow it to drip on yourself.

Shortbread cookies with fresh cream and fruit

This easy-to-assemble dessert is a wicked union of sweet red fruits and luscious whipped cream, anchored in rounds of lemon-tinged shortbread cookies.

Preparation time **45 minutes + refrigeration**
Total cooking time **20–25 minutes**
Serves 4–6

SHORTBREAD COOKIES
1 1/4 cups unsalted butter, at room temperature
1 1/4 cups confectioners' sugar
finely grated rind of 1 lemon
vanilla extract
1 egg, lightly beaten
3 1/2 cups all-purpose flour, sifted

FILLING
3/4 cup heavy cream
1 teaspoon vanilla extract
sugar, to taste
1 cup assorted red fruits, such as strawberries,
   raspberries and red currants

1/3 cup confectioners' sugar, to dust

1 Brush two baking sheets with melted butter and refrigerate. Preheat the oven to 325°F. To make the pastry, beat the butter and sugar until pale and smooth. Stir in the rind and a few drops of vanilla. Add the egg gradually, beating well after each addition. Add the flour in one batch and stir until combined: the mixture will be very soft and sticky.

2 Divide the mixture in half. Roll out each portion 1/8 inch thick between two sheets of well-floured waxed paper, working quickly and lightly. Place on the baking sheets with the paper attached. Refrigerate until firm.

3 Slide the pastry off the sheets onto a work surface. Remove the top piece of paper, dip a 31/2-inch fluted cookie-cutter in flour and cut three cookies per serving. Ease the cookies off the bottom sheet of paper onto the baking sheets and pierce with a fork. Bake for 20–25 minutes, or until golden; cool briefly before removing from the baking sheet to cool on a rack.

4 To make the filling, pour the cream into a bowl, add the vanilla, and sugar to taste. Whisk into soft peaks. (Do not overwhisk as the cream will overthicken and separate.) Spoon into a pastry bag fitted with a star nozzle.

5 To assemble, pipe some cream onto the middle of a cookie; arrange some fruit around the cream (but not over the edge). Top with another cookie, repeat with more cream and fruit, then top with a third cookie. Dust with the sifted confectioners' sugar. Finish the remaining rounds, reserving some fruit. Transfer to serving plates and decorate with the reserved fruit.

Banana tartes Tatin

This recipe is a variation of the classic tarte Tatin, *using bananas in place of the apples.*

Preparation time **35 minutes + 20 minutes refrigeration**
Total cooking time **40 minutes**
Makes 4

2/3 cup sugar
1/4 teaspoon lemon juice
4 bananas
1/2 quantity short pastry (see page 58)

1 Preheat the oven to 325°F. Place four 4-inch wide, 11/4-inch deep well-greased pot pie or cake pans on a baking sheet and chill.

2 Place a shallow pan half filled with cold water next to the stove. Place the sugar and 3 tablespoons water in a small heavy-bottomed saucepan and stir until the sugar dissolves. Bring to a boil, add the lemon juice and cook, without stirring, until the mixture is golden. Dip the bottom of the saucepan in the cold water to stop the cooking process, then remove the pan from the water immediately. Divide the caramel between the molds, turning them to cover the bottoms evenly. The caramel will harden, so work quickly before it sets, but be careful as the molds may get very hot.

3 Peel the bananas, remove the ends, and cut into 3/4-inch thick slices. Arrange cut-side-down in the prepared molds, packing as tightly as possible.

4 Roll out the pastry to just over 1/8 inch thick and cut four rounds the same diameter as the molds. Place a pastry round on top of each tart and pierce with a fork. Refrigerate for 20 minutes. Bake for 30 minutes, or until the pastry is cooked and golden. Unmold the tartlets onto plates and serve hot.

Pithiviers

This pastry originated in the town of Pithiviers in central France. It is the traditional cake served on Epiphany, January 6th, when a bean is added to it. The guest who gets the bean becomes king or queen for the day. During the winter holidays, these cakes can be seen adorned with gold crowns in French bakeries.

Preparation time **45 minutes + refrigeration**
Total cooking time **40 minutes**
Serves 4–6

I quantity puff pastry (see pages 60–61)
I egg, beaten, to glaze
2 tablespoons sugar

ALMOND CREAM
3 tablespoons unsalted butter, softened
3 tablespoons sugar
1/4 cup ground almonds
I egg
2 teaspoons all-purpose flour
2 teaspoons rum

1 Preheat the oven to 425°F. Cut the puff pastry in half and roll into two 8-inch squares. Place on wax paper-lined baking sheets and chill.

2 To make the almond cream, beat the butter and sugar together, add the almonds and egg and mix well. Stir in the flour, then the rum. Chill.

3 Remove one of the baking sheets of pastry from the refrigerator. Using a plate or large round pastry ring, make a light imprint on the pastry 5 1/2 inches in diameter. Brush around the imprint with the beaten egg. Place the almond cream in the center and spread it into a dome, taking care not to touch the glazed dough. Place the second piece of pastry over the first and press the edges to seal.

4 Using the tip of a teaspoon, gently press around the edge of the pastry to make small, uniform semicircles—creating a scalloped effect. Chill for 10 minutes, then use a small sharp knife to cut away the pattern marked by the spoon. Preheat the oven to 400°F.

5 Make a syrup by mixing the sugar with 2 tablespoons water in a small saucepan. Stir over medium heat until the sugar dissolves, then bring to a boil. Remove from the heat and cool.

6 Brush the pastry with the egg glaze, without letting any drip down the sides, as this will prevent the pastry from rising properly. Using the tip of a small knife, score the top of the pastry in a spiral pattern. Bake for 10 minutes, then reduce the heat to 350°F and bake for 25 minutes more, or until golden brown. Remove from the oven and immediately brush the top with the syrup to give it a shine. Serve the pithiviers warm.

Apricot tart

This delicious tart uses the classic combination of fruit and almond cream and may be made all year round, using canned fruit when fresh apricots are out of season. The results will always be excellent.

Preparation time **25 minutes + refrigeration**
Cooking time **1 hour 10 minutes**
Serves **6–8**

🎖 🎖

1 sheet frozen puff pastry, thawed
1/3 cup toasted sliced almonds
6 oz. apricot halves, fresh or canned and well drained
2 tablespoons apricot jam

ALMOND CREAM
3 tablespoons unsalted butter, at room temperature
3 tablespoons sugar
1 egg, lightly beaten
1/4 cup ground almonds
1 tablespoon all-purpose flour
1–2 teaspoons rum

1 Brush a shallow, 8-inch fluted tart pan with removable bottom, with melted butter. Preheat the oven to 425°F.

2 Roll out the pastry sheet on a floured surface into a thin circle large enough to fit the prepared pan. Line the tart pan (see Chef's techniques, page 63), then chill for 30 minutes. Bake blind for 20 minutes, then remove the weights and paper and bake for a further 8 minutes (see

Chef's techniques, page 63). As the pastry cools, gently press it down with a dish towel. Reduce the oven temperature to 350°F.

3 To make the almond cream, beat the butter and sugar together using a wooden spoon or electric mixer, until light and pale. Gradually add the egg, a third at a time, beating well after each addition. Stir in the ground almonds, flour and rum.

4 Sprinkle the sliced almonds over the bottom of the pastry shell. Spread or pipe the almond cream over them, smoothing the surface using the back of a spoon that has been dipped in water. Arrange the apricot halves, cut-side-down, over the almond cream.

5 Bake for 35–40 minutes, or until the almond cream is light golden and puffed. Carefully remove the tart from the pan and cool on a wire rack.

6 Melt the apricot jam and 1 tablespoon water in a small saucepan until smooth, then strain. Reheat if the glaze cools and thickens before you use it. Brush a thin layer of the glaze over the surface of the cooled tart, taking care not to go over the same area twice. Serve the tart cold.

Chef's tip Sprinkling sliced almonds over the bottom of the pastry provides an added crunch and prevents the pastry from becoming soggy.

Treacle tart

This English dessert can be served hot or cold and is delicious accompanied by either a warm stirred custard or vanilla ice cream.

*Preparation time **40 minutes + 30 minutes refrigeration***
*Total cooking time **1 hour***
Serves 8

❀ ❀

1 quantity short pastry (see page 58)
1 egg, beaten with 1 egg yolk, to glaze

FILLING
1 1/4 cups golden syrup (see Chef's tip)
2/3 cup heavy cream
1 egg
finely grated rind of 1 lemon
1/4 cup ground almonds
1 cup fresh bread crumbs

1 Grease a 1-inch deep, 8-inch fluted tart pan with removable base, with butter.
2 Roll out two thirds of the pastry on a floured surface to a circle about 1/8-inch thick. Line the pan (see Chef's techniques, page 63) and chill for about 30 minutes. Preheat the oven to 400°F. Bake blind for 10–15 minutes until firm. Remove the weights and paper (see Chef's techniques, page 63) and cool. Reduce the oven temperature to 350°F.
3 To prepare the lattice top, roll out the remaining pastry to 1/8-inch thick. Cut strips of pastry 5/8-inch wide and long enough to reach across the tart. Refrigerate while preparing the filling.
4 To make the filling, place the syrup in a saucepan and heat gently until warm. In a bowl, mix together the cream and egg. Add the lemon rind and warm syrup and stir to blend. In a separate bowl, mix together the ground almonds and bread crumbs, make a well in the center and pour in the liquid. Slowly incorporate the dry ingredients until the mixture is smooth. Pour into the prepared pastry shell, filling to just below the rim.
5 Brush the rim of the pastry shell with the egg glaze. Wipe off any splashes on the tart pan because they will stick and make the tart difficult to remove. Beginning in the center and working outwards, lay half the pastry strips on the surface of the tart, 5/8 inch apart. Cut off at the edges by pressing down with your thumbs. Place the second layer of strips on the diagonal, again starting in the center, to create a lattice pattern. Brush with the remaining glaze. Bake for 25–35 minutes, or until golden brown. Cool slightly before removing from the pan.

Chef's tip Golden syrup is also called light treacle. To find out where to obtain it, call the publisher at (800) 526-2778. You can also substitute dark corn syrup, but the flavor will be different.

Saint-Honoré

During the Middle Ages, most pastries were produced by the clergy, hence the religious names or connotations they still have today. Saint Honoré is the patron saint of pastry-makers.

Preparation time **1 hour + 30 minutes chilling**
Total cooking time **1 hour 30 minutes**
Serves 6–8

1/2 quantity sweet pastry (see page 59)
I quantity cream-puff pastry (see page 62)
I egg, beaten, to glaze
I cup sugar

CHANTILLY CREAM
3/4 cup whipping cream, chilled
1/3 cup confectioners' sugar
I teaspoon vanilla extract

1 Preheat the oven to 350°F. Grease two baking sheets with melted butter and chill. Lightly flour the work surface and roll the pastry out to 1/8-inch thick. Cut out a circle 8 inches in diameter for the base of the Saint-Honoré. Place on one of the chilled baking sheets, pierce with a fork and brush lightly with beaten egg.

2 Spoon the cream-puff pastry into a pastry bag fitted with a large 1/2-inch pastry nozzle and pipe a ring of cream puff pastry around the edge of the sweet pastry, about the same thickness as the sweet pastry. Pipe another ring inside the first one, touching the outer ring, and brush with the egg. Bake for 40 minutes, or until the pastry is well browned and the cream-puff pastry well puffed. Do not open the oven door for the first 15 minutes or the cream-puff pastry will collapse. Cool on a wire rack.

3 On the other chilled baking sheet, pipe small balls of cream-puff pastry, the size of walnuts, leaving a space of at least 2 inches between them. Glaze with the beaten egg and smooth the tops so they are uniform. Bake for 40 minutes, or until the balls are well browned and puffed. Remove from the oven and cool on a wire rack.

4 To make the caramel, fill a shallow pan with cold water and place it next to the stove. Place the sugar and 1/4 cup water in a small, heavy-based saucepan. Stir over low heat to dissolve the sugar, then bring to a boil and simmer until the caramel takes on a light golden color. Stop the cooking by placing the bottom of the saucepan into the pan of cold water for a few seconds. Working quickly, carefully dip one side of the cream-puff pastry balls into the caramel and allow to cool on a buttered baking sheet for 2 minutes. Then dip the cream-puff pastry balls in again, on the other side, and quickly lay, at regular intervals, around the edge of the Saint-Honoré base.

5 To make the Chantilly cream, pour the cream into a bowl and add the sugar and vanilla. Using a whisk or electric mixer, beat the cream until it forms soft peaks.

6 Place the cream in a pastry bag fitted with a large star nozzle, then fill the center of the bottom. Refrigerate for at least 30 minutes before serving.

Rhubarb pastry

*This dessert or brunch treat has a light and crisp puff pastry base, topped with a
delicious combination of sharp fruit and sweet crumbs.*

Preparation time 30 minutes + 20 minutes chilling
Total cooking time 1 hour 20 minutes
Serves 6

1 quantity puff pastry (see pages 60–61)
1 egg, beaten, to glaze
1 tablespoon honey
10 oz. fresh or frozen rhubarb, chopped
2 tablespoons sugar
pinch of ground cinnamon
confectioners' sugar, to dust

TOPPING
1/4 cup unsalted butter
2/3 cup all-purpose flour
2 1/2 tablespoons sugar

ALMOND CREAM
1/3 cup unsalted butter, at room temperature
1/3 cup sugar
finely grated rind of 1/2 lemon
1 egg, lightly beaten
1/3 cup ground almonds
1 tablespoon all-purpose flour

1 Roll out two-thirds of the pastry on a lightly floured
surface to make a 9 1/2-inch square. Place on a wax
paper-lined baking sheet and trim the edges with a large
sharp knife. Roll out the remaining pastry to a rectangle
about 9 x 3 1/2 inches and 1/4-inch thick. Cut four
8 1/2 x 3/4 inch-strips from this rectangle. Brush the top
of the square with the beaten egg, making sure that it
does not drip down the sides because this will set during
baking and cause the pastry to rise unevenly. Without
stretching the strips, place them carefully on the edges
of the square to make a border. Score crosshatch marks
on the border using the back of a knife, then brush
lightly with the egg. Chill for 20 minutes.

2 Melt the honey in a saucepan over medium heat. Add
the rhubarb, sugar and cinnamon and cook, uncovered,
over low heat for 20 minutes, or until the fruit is soft,
shaking the pan occasionally to prevent the rhubarb
from sticking. The rhubarb should have a slightly acidic
flavor, however, it may be necessary to add a little extra
sugar. Let cool in the pan. Preheat the oven to 400°F.

3 Remove the pastry from the refrigerator. Using a fork,
pierce all over the square bottom inside the border to keep
it from rising as it cooks. Bake for 10–15 minutes (the
border should rise and the center should be fairly flat).

4 To make the topping, use your fingertips to rub the
butter into the flour until it resembles bread crumbs,
then add the sugar. The mixture should have a coarse,
crumbly texture.

5 To make the almond cream, use a wooden spoon or
electric mixer to cream the butter, sugar and lemon rind
together until light and pale. Add the egg gradually,
beating well after each addition. Stir in the ground
almonds and flour. Spread the almond cream over the
bottom of the precooked pastry, and spoon the cooled
rhubarb mixture on top. Sprinkle the topping over the
rhubarb and bake for 40 minutes. Carefully lift or slide
the pastry off the baking sheet onto a wire rack to cool.
Dust with sifted confectioners' sugar just before serving.

Congress tarts

These small tarts are a delight to make and are delicious served slightly warm or cold with tea or coffee.

*Preparation time **30 minutes + 10 minutes refrigeration***
*Total cooking time **20 minutes***
Makes 18

1/2 quantity sweet pastry (see page 59)
1 cup sugar
3/4 cup ground almonds
2 tablespoons rice flour or fine semolina
pinch of ground cinnamon
3 egg whites
3/4 cup flaked or finely shredded coconut (see Chef's tip)
finely grated rind of 1/2 lemon
1/4 cup raspberry jam

1   Brush two deep 12-hole, 1 1/4 fl. oz. capacity, 2 1/2-inch tartlet or mini muffin pans with melted butter. Preheat the oven to 400°F.

2   On a lightly floured surface, roll out the pastry about 1/4-inch thick. Cut out 18 rounds using a 2 3/4-inch fluted cutter and line the pans. Place on a baking sheet and refrigerate for 10 minutes.

3   Sift the sugar, ground almonds, rice flour or semolina and cinnamon into a large bowl. In a separate bowl, whisk the egg whites until foamy but still liquid and fold in the sifted ingredients. Stir in 1/2 cup of the coconut and the lemon rind.

4   Place a little jam in the bottom of each pastry shell, without spreading it. Spoon in the coconut filling to three-quarters full and sprinkle with the remaining coconut. Bake for 20 minutes, or until golden brown and firm. Cool before removing from the pans.

Chef's tip If using sweetened coconut, reduce the sugar to 3/4 cup.

Danish pastries

*Although this recipe may be time-consuming, nothing quite matches the taste of this freshly made
rich and flaky yeast dough.*

*Preparation time 2 hours 15 minutes + refrigeration
    + 30 minutes rising*
Total cooking time 30 minutes
Makes 28

2 lb. bread or all-purpose flour
1/3 cup sugar
4 teaspoons salt
1 oz. fresh yeast or 1/2 oz. dry yeast
3 cups warm milk
14 oz. unsalted butter, chilled

PASTRY CREAM
2 cups milk
1/2 vanilla bean, split lengthwise
5 egg yolks
1/2 cup sugar
2 1/2 tablespoons all-purpose flour
2 1/2 tablespoons cornstarch

3 x 16 oz. cans apricot halves, drained
1 egg, beaten
2/3 cup sliced almonds
3 tablespoons apricot jam

1 Butter and flour a baking sheet. Sift the flour, sugar
and salt into a large bowl and make a well in the center.
Cream the yeast with 1/4 cup of the warm milk. Stir in
the remaining milk and pour into the well. Gradually
incorporate the flour into the yeast mixture with your
fingers to make a soft dough. Knead the dough on a
floured surface until smooth and elastic. Cover with
plastic wrap and chill for 10 minutes.

2 To make the pastry cream, place the milk and vanilla
bean in a saucepan and bring to a boil. In a bowl, whisk
the egg yolks and sugar until light in color. Sift in the
flour and cornstarch and whisk until blended. Remove
and discard the vanilla bean. Pour half the boiling milk
into the yolk mixture, whisk well, then return the
mixture to the saucepan of milk. Bring to a boil, stirring
constantly, and boil for 1 minute to completely cook the
flour. Remove from the heat and spread the pastry
cream on a tray to cool quickly. Cover the surface with
wax paper to prevent a skin from forming.

3 On a floured surface, roll out the dough into a
rectangle three times as long as it is wide, and 1/8-inch
thick. Press and roll out the butter between two long
sheets of plastic wrap into a rectangle, the same width
as, but two-thirds the length of, the dough. Unwrap and
lay the butter on the top two-thirds of the dough. Fold
the exposed third of the dough up over the butter and
fold the top third down.

4 Turn the dough to look like a book, with the binding
on the left, and roll again into a rectangle and fold into
three. Repeat twice, wrapping in plastic wrap and
chilling for 20 minutes between each roll.

5 On a floured surface, roll the dough out into a
rectangle or square 1/8-inch thick. Cut into 4-inch
squares and place on the prepared baking sheet. Preheat
the oven to 400°F.

6 Pipe the pastry cream into the center of each square
and top with two apricot halves. Brush one corner with
the beaten egg and bring up that corner and the
opposite one to touch between the apricots. Press firmly
in the center. Let rest in a warm place to rise for
30 minutes. Brush with the egg and sprinkle with the
almonds. Bake for 15–20 minutes, or until golden. Cool
on wire racks.

7 Melt the apricot jam with 1 tablespoon water and
then strain. Brush the tops of the apricots with the hot
apricot glaze and serve.

Tarte grand-mère

This tart, with its slightly caramelized, nutty flavor, will delight friends and family whether served at a coffee break or at the end of a meal.

Preparation time *50 minutes + 15 minutes refrigeration*
Total cooking time *1 hour 20 minutes*
Serves 6–8

1 quantity short pastry (see page 58)

FILLING
2 tablespoons unsalted butter
2 tablespoons sugar
1 large apple, about 6 oz., peeled, seeded and cubed
1/2 cup shelled pistachios
1/2 cup chopped walnuts
pinch of ground cinnamon
3 egg yolks
2 1/2 tablespoons sugar
1 tablespoon vanilla sugar (see Chef's tip)
2/3 cup whipping cream
confectioners' sugar, to dust
extra chopped walnuts, to garnish

1 Preheat the oven to 350°F. Brush a 1-inch deep, 9-inch fluted tart pan with removable bottom, with melted butter. On a lightly floured surface, roll out the pastry 1/8 inch thick. Line the tart pan (see Chef's techniques, page 63) and refrigerate for 15 minutes.

2 Melt the butter and sugar in a nonstick skillet over medium heat. When the mixture is lightly colored, add the apple and sauté for 3 minutes. Add the nuts, transfer to a bowl and sprinkle with the cinnamon. Let cool.

3 In a bowl, whisk together the egg yolks, sugar and vanilla sugar. Whisk in the cream, then strain the mixture through a sieve.

4 Remove the pastry shell from the refrigerator and bake blind for 10 minutes until firm. Remove the weights and paper and bake for 15 minutes more, or until the pastry is lightly colored (see Chef's techniques, page 63). Transfer to a wire rack to cool.

5 Spread the apple mixture over the bottom of the pastry shell and pour in the egg mixture. Bake for 40–45 minutes, or until golden brown and set. Let cool slightly on a wire rack before removing from the pan. Serve warm, dusted with sifted confectioners' sugar and sprinkled with extra chopped walnuts.

Chef's tip It is easy to make your own vanilla sugar. Just place a fresh vanilla bean inside a jar of sugar. Seal well and use whenever required.

Chef's techniques

◆

Short pastry

*This delicious dough produces one of the most versatile pastries for tarts and
is also one of the easiest to make.*

*Preparation time **10 minutes + 20 minutes chilling***
*Total cooking time **None***
Makes about 1 lb

1²/3 cups all-purpose flour
large pinch of salt
large pinch of sugar
1/3 cup unsalted butter, chilled
1 egg, lightly beaten
1–2 drops vanilla extract

1   In a large bowl, sift together the flour, salt and sugar.
Cut the butter into 1/2-inch cubes and add to the flour.
2   Rub the butter into the flour using your fingertips
until the mixture resembles fine bread crumbs.
3   Make a well in the center and pour in the combined
egg, 2–3 teaspoons water and the vanilla.
4   Slowly work the mixture together with a fork or
flexible metal spatula until it makes a rough ball. If it is
slightly sticky, add a little more flour. Turn out onto a
lightly floured cool surface, shape the dough into a ball
and flatten it slightly. Wrap the pastry in plastic wrap
and chill for 20 minutes before using.

Chef's tip This quantity of pastry is enough to line two
shallow 8–9 inch tart pans. If only making one tart,
divide the pastry in half and wrap separately in plastic
wrap. Use one piece and put the second one in a plastic
bag and seal, airtight, to freeze and use another time.

*Add the cubes of butter to the
flour and salt, and rub into the
dry ingredients.*

*Continue rubbing the butter into
the flour until the mixture
resembles fine bread crumbs.*

*Pour the combined egg, water
and vanilla into the well in the
dry ingredients.*

*Slowly work the mixture
together with a metal spatula
until it makes a rough ball.*

Sweet pastry

This pastry is made in a similar way to the short pastry, but has added sugar for when a tart needs a little extra sweetness.

*Preparation time **10 minutes + 20 minutes chilling***
*Total cooking time **None***
Makes about 1 lb

1²/₃ cups all-purpose flour
large pinch of salt
¹/₄ cup unsalted butter
¹/₃ cup sugar
1 egg, lightly beaten
1–2 drops vanilla extract

1 In a large bowl, sift together the flour and salt. Cut the butter into 1/2-inch cubes and add to the flour. Rub the butter into the flour using your fingertips until the mixture resembles fine bread crumbs.

2 Stir in the sugar and make a well in the center. Pour in the combined egg and vanilla and slowly work the mixture together using a fork or flexible metal spatula. If the dough is too dry, sprinkle it with a little water until it just holds together.

3 Remove the dough from the bowl to a lightly floured surface. Using the palm of your hand, smear the dough away from you until it is smooth.

4 Gather the dough into a ball and flatten it slightly. Wrap in plastic wrap and place in the refrigerator to chill for 20 minutes before using.

Chef's tip This quantity of pastry is enough to line two shallow 8–9 inch tart pans. If only making one tart, divide the pastry in half and wrap separately in plastic wrap. Use one piece and put the second one in a plastic bag and seal, airtight, to freeze and use another time.

Sift the flour and salt into a large bowl. Cut the butter into small cubes and rub into the flour.

Stir in the sugar. Make a well in the center of the dry ingredients and add the combined egg and vanilla.

Using the palm of your hand, smear the dough away from you on a lightly floured surface several times until smooth.

Shape the dough into a ball and flatten slightly.

Puff pastry

This pastry requires more effort and time than the other pastries, but the result is a lovely buttery and flaky base for any tart or pastry. If you are short of time, purchased sheets of puff pastry are a good alternative.

Preparation time **1 day**
Total cooking time **None**
Makes about 1 lb.

DOUGH BASE
2 cups bread or all-purpose flour
I teaspoon salt
2–3 drops of lemon juice
¹/2 cup water
3 tablespoons unsalted butter, melted

¹/3 cup unsalted butter, chilled

1 To make the dough base, sift the flour and salt onto a cool work surface and make a well in the center. Add the lemon juice to the water, then place in the well with the butter and mix together with your fingertips. With the side of a metal spatula, use a cutting action to incorporate the flour into the butter mixture until the flour disappears and the mixture resembles loose crumbs. Bring the dough together with your hands and knead lightly, adding a few drops of water if necessary, to form a smooth soft ball.

2 Cut an "X" in the top of the ball to prevent shrinkage, then wrap in lightly floured wax paper or plastic wrap. Chill for 1 hour—this will make the dough more pliable for rolling. Place the chilled butter between two pieces of wax paper or plastic wrap. Tap it with the side of a rolling pin and shape into a 3/4-inch thick square. This action will make the butter pliable to roll, without melting it.

3 Unwrap the dough and place it on a lightly floured cool surface. Roll the dough from just off center to shape a cross with a mound in the center.

4 Place the butter on the mound and fold the four sides of dough over the butter to enclose it completely.

Sift the flour and salt onto a work surface and make a well in the center. Add the lemon juice, water and butter and blend together with your fingertips.

Cut an "X" on top of the pastry with a sharp knife.

Unwrap the chilled dough and place it on a lightly floured surface. Roll from just off center to form a cross shape with a mound in the center.

Place the butter on the central mound and fold the four sides of the dough up over the butter to enclose it.

5 Roll over the top and bottom of the dough to seal the edges. On a lightly floured surface, roll the dough into a 5 x 14-inch rectangle.

6 Fold into a stack of three layers by folding the bottom third up over the middle and the top third down. Brush off the excess flour and make sure that the edges all meet neatly. Make an indentation with your finger to record the first roll and fold. Wrap in plastic wrap and chill for 30 minutes.

7 Give the dough a quarter turn with the folded side on your left as if it was a book. With a rolling pin, gently press down to seal the edges.

8 Repeat steps 5–7 three more times, remembering to record each roll with an indentation and chilling for 30 minutes after each roll. After two rolls and folds, you should have two indentations. The finished pastry should have four indentations, and will start to look smoother as you continue to roll and fold. Let the dough rest in the refrigerator for a final 30 minutes. The puff pastry is now ready to use. It can be frozen whole, or cut into smaller portions, then used as needed.

Chef's tips When making puff pastry, work on a cool surface to prevent the butter from melting and forming a heavy dough. In hot weather, it may be necessary to refrigerate the dough for an extra 15 minutes during the final resting.

Making puff pastry is not difficult, but it is time consuming, so make two or three quantities at once and freeze the extra. Thaw the pastry by leaving it overnight in the refrigerator. Puff pastry will keep in the refrigerator for 4 days and in the freezer for 3 months.

Seal the edges of the dough by pressing down with a rolling pin. Roll the pastry into a rectangle.

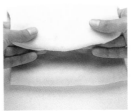

Fold the dough into a stack of three layers by folding the bottom third up over the middle and the top third down.

After chilling the dough, put it on the surface in front of you as before and turn it a quarter turn so that it looks like a book with the binding on the left. Press down to seal the edges, then roll, fold and chill again.

Continue rolling, folding and chilling, trying to maintain an even finish and neat corners.

Cream-puff pastry

This pastry is cooked twice to give the lightness found in éclairs and cream-puffs. Before the final baking, the dough is fairly wet and needs to be piped.

*Preparation time **5 minutes***
*Total cooking time **10–15 minutes***

²/₃ cup all-purpose flour
3 tablespoons unsalted butter, cubed
pinch of salt
2 teaspoons sugar
2 eggs

1 Sift the flour onto a clean sheet of waxed paper. Place 1/2 cup water, the butter, salt and sugar in a saucepan. Heat until the butter and water come to a boil. Remove from the heat and add the flour all at once.
2 Mix well using a wooden spoon. Return to the heat and mix until a smooth ball forms and the dough leaves the sides of the pan.
3 Remove from the heat and place the dough in a bowl. Lightly beat the eggs in a small bowl. Using a wooden spoon or electric mixer, add the eggs to the dough a little at a time, beating well after each addition.
4 The mixture is ready to use when it is smooth, thick and glossy.

Chef's tips It is essential when making cream-puff pastry to measure the ingredients carefully, as too much moisture can cause them to collapse. Traditionally, bakers weigh the eggs in order to determine the weight of the dry ingredients.

Don't be fooled by golden colored cream-puff pastry! If the cracks of the pastry are still light yellow or much lighter than the rest of the pastry, it indicates the interior is not quite cooked. Reduce the temperature to 325°F and continue baking.

Once boiling, remove the water, butter, salt and sugar mixture from the heat and stir in the sifted flour.

Return the pan to the heat and cook until the mixture forms a smooth ball that comes away from the sides of the pan.

Remove from the heat and transfer the mixture to a bowl. Gradually beat in the eggs with a wooden spoon.

The mixture is ready to use when it is smooth, thick and glossy.

Lining a tart pan

Be very careful when handling the dough to avoid stretching it.

Place the dough over a rolling pin and unroll loosely over the pan.

Press the sides of the pastry into the flutes or sides of the pan by using a small ball of excess pastry.

Use a rolling pin to trim the pastry edges. Gently but firmly roll across the top of the pan. Refrigerate for 10 minutes.

Pierce the pastry shell all over with a fork to let steam escape during baking.

Baking blind

Baking the pastry before adding the filling prevents the bottom from becoming soggy during cooking.

Crush a sheet of waxed paper lightly into a ball. Open out the paper, then lay it inside the pastry shell.

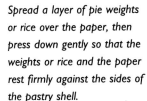

Spread a layer of pie weights or rice over the paper, then press down gently so that the weights or rice and the paper rest firmly against the sides of the pastry shell.

Bake according to the time specified in the recipe, or until firm. Remove the weights or rice and paper.

If indicated in the recipe, continue baking until the pastry looks dry and is evenly colored.

First published in the United States in 1998 by Periplus Editions (HK) Ltd., with editorial offices at
153 Milk Street, Boston, Massachusetts 02109.

Murdoch Books and Le Cordon Bleu thank the 32 masterchefs of all the Le Cordon Bleu Schools, whose knowledge and
expertise have made this book possible, especially: Chef Cliche (MOF), Chef Terrien, Chef Boucheret, Chef Duchêne (MOF),
Chef Guillut, Chef Steneck, Paris; Chef Males, Chef Walsh, Chef Hardy, London; Chef Chantefort, Chef Bertin, Chef Jambert,
Chef Honda, Tokyo; Chef Salembien, Chef Boutin, Chef Harris, Sydney; Chef Lawes, Adelaide; Chef Guiet, Chef Denis, Ottawa.
Of the many students who helped the Chefs test each recipe, a special mention to graduates David Welch and Allen Wertheim.
A very special acknowledgment to Directors Susan Eckstein, Great Britain, and Kathy Shaw, Paris, who have been responsible for
the coordination of the Le Cordon Bleu team throughout this series.

The Publisher and Le Cordon Bleu also wish to thank Carole Sweetnam for her help with this series.

First published in Australia in 1998 by Murdoch Books®

Managing Editor: Kay Halsey
Series Concept, Design and Art Direction: Juliet Cohen
Editor: Elizabeth Cotton
Food Director: Jody Vassallo
Food Editors: Dimitra Stais, Tracy Rutherford
US Editor: Linda Venturoni Wilson
Designer: Annette Fitzgerald
Photographers: André Martin, Chris Jones, Luis Martin
Food Stylists: Jane Hann, Carolyn Fienberg, Mary Harris
Food Preparation: Kathy Knudsen, Kerrie Mullins, Justine Poole, Kerrie Ray
Chef's Techniques Photographer: Reg Morrison
Home Economists: Joanna Beaumont, Michelle Earl, Michelle Lawton, Kerrie Mullins, Angela Nahas, Kerrie Ray, Alison Turner

Library of Congress catalog card number: 98-65973
ISBN 962-593-436-7

Front cover: Orange tart

Distributed in the United States by
Charles E. Tuttle Co., Inc.
RR1 Box 231-5
North Clarendon, VT 05759
Tel: (802) 773-8930
Fax: (802) 773-6993

Printed in Singapore

05 04 03 02 01 00 99 98 10 9 8 7 6 5 4 3 2 1

Important: Some of the recipes in this book may include raw eggs, which can cause salmonella poisoning.
Those who might be at risk from this (the elderly, pregnant women, young children and those suffering
from immune deficiency diseases) should check with their physicians before eating raw eggs.